LEIF ERIKSSON

His Forgotten Discovery of America

Written by Julie Lorang
In collaboration with Thomas Jacquemin
Translated by Rose Brichard

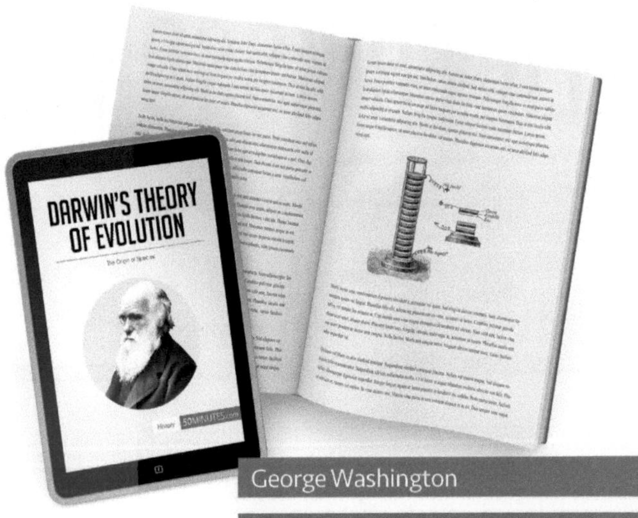

LEIF ERIKSSON

KEY INFORMATION

- **Born:** circa 970, probably in Iceland
- **Died:** circa 1020, probably in Greenland
- **Expedition aims:**
  - Founding a new colony
  - Finding new wealth and resources
- **Regions of the world explored:** the Labrador and Newfoundland coasts, Canada
- **Most notable discovery:** the Americas, almost 500 years before Christopher Columbus

Leif Eriksson (sometimes spelled Leif Ericson or Leif Erikkson) was a Viking navigator who made a name for himself in both Iceland and Greenland. He is thought to have discovered the Americas at the turn of first millennium AD, almost 500 years before Christopher Columbus (Genoese navigator, 1450/1451-1506).

The Vikings were first and foremost great explorers and merchants, contrary to popular belief which portrays them as warlords who looted and pillaged wherever they went. They established colonies in Europe, around the Mediterranean, all along the coast of the Black Sea and even as far afield as North America. As explorers, they were centuries ahead the rest of Europe due to their technologically superior ships capable of sailing the oceans and not just the seas, along with their acute sense of direction, developed and passed down through the generations. Through this, the Vikings were able to venture into undiscovered and unexplored lands.

Along with his crew, Leif Eriksson discovered Vinland, a fertile land rich in natural resources in North-East Canada on Newfoundland Island. The Vikings settled there for several years before being forced to give up their land and wealth due to conflict with the Native American population. Despite how extraordinary this discovery was given the era in which it occurred, it was largely forgotten for almost nine centuries until historians and archaeologists took new interest in Norse sagas, which tell the impressive tale of Eriksson, the great explorer.

BIOGRAPHY

Statue of Leif Eriksson in Qassiarsuk, in the South of Greeland.

LEIF ERIKSSON: A LIFE TOLD THROUGH NORSE SAGAS

Our only source on Leif Eriksson's life and career are the Norse sagas. These texts are written in prose and relay the highlights and great events in the lives of some of the great figures of Vikingdom. For several generations, the stories were passed down orally and transformed before being recorded in written form around 1250. Two of these sagas give us an insight into Leif Eriksson's life and discoveries:

- the Saga of Erik the Red
- the Greenland Saga

These two texts contain vital information, despite the fact that their accounts of events occasionally differ and contradict one another.

CHILDHOOD IN EXILE

It is thought that Leif Eriksson was born around 970 in Iceland. His parents were Thjodhild and Erik the Red (Erik Thorvaldsson, circa 930-1003), a man who owes this title to his red hair. Erik the Red's father was exiled from Norway for the violent crimes committed by his own father Thorvald Asvaldsson, and the family settled in Iceland.

Ten years later, history repeated itself when Erik the Red killed a group of Icelandic people in the wake of a dispute between them. The family was once again banished and headed westward to try their luck further afield. This led

Erik the Red to discover the South of Greenland, and he established the first European colony there. Hoping to attract more settlers, Erik the Red named the island Greenland, despite its Arctic climate. The young Leif Eriksson therefore became the son of the richest and most feared man in the small Greenland colony.

DISCOVERING CHRISTIANITY

As a young man, Leif Eriksson set out on a voyage which took him to the Scottish Hebrides, a group of islands situated to the north west of mainland Scotland, and to Norway, his homeland. During his journey, he met a noblewoman named Thorgunna and had a son with her, whom they named Thorgils.

He then went to the court of the Norwegian King Olaf I (circa 963-1000) and became one of his closest knights. Eriksson was strongly influenced by the King, who had taken it upon himself to spread Christianity to the whole of Norway. He renounced the Pagan gods he had previously worshipped and became a Christian convert.

At King Olaf's request, Eriksson agreed to take a team of Christian missionaries to Greenland to spread their beliefs. In Greenland, he led construction on the country's first church. This was much to his father's dissatisfaction, as Greenland was still largely attached to ancient gods and beliefs.

THE RUMOUR AT THE HEART OF ERIKSSON'S EXPEDITION

Around the year 1000, Leif Eriksson learned of a rumour which was circulating among the little Greenland colony. A man named Bjarni Herjolfsson (Icelandic explorer, circa 965-1000) had apparently lost his way at sea while fishing somewhere between Greenland and Iceland. His ship had been blown off course and, rumour had it, this had led him to catch sight of unfamiliar land on the horizon. Eriksson was intrigued and decided to set off in search of this new territory himself, with the help of information from Herjolfsson who had eventually made it safely home.

Eriksson set off towards the west with a crew of 35 men and quickly came across the land in question which he procee-ded to name Vinland, part of modern day Newfoundland, Canada. Eriksson therefore became the first European to set foot on the American continent, long before Columbus did so in 1492. Despite this new land being fertile and abundant in resources, Eriksson only spent a few months there before going back to Greenland. This is perhaps because he was to take over as head of the colony from his father.

Painting showing Leif Eriksson just as he discovers Vinland.

A few years later in around 1020, Eriksson died in the company of family and friends. It is thought that he left everything to his second son Thorkell.

POLITICAL, SOCIAL AND ECONOMIC CONTEXT

Eriksson's remarkable discovery, almost half a century before Christopher Columbus would take credit for the same feat, was only made possible by the highly developed Norse navigation technology. This expertise and prowess in the area of exploration, with which the rest of Europe could not compete at the time, departs markedly from the place Vikings often hold in the collective imagination.

DID YOU SAY VIKING?

The Vikings, also known as Norse people (which literally means men of the North), were populations of explorers, merchants and pirates who lived between the 9th and 11th centuries. They were originally from Scandinavia (Denmark, Norway and Sweden) but colonised large parts of Europe, the Mediterranean, the Black Sea coastline and even North America.

The word Viking has its origin in Old Norse, the ancient language of Scandinavia and Iceland, and links to the maritime expeditions undertaken by these well-seasoned navigators.

Historians class the Viking Age as the centuries (circa 700 to 1100 AD) during which many Vikings left Scandinavia in search of their fortune and new lands. The Viking Age came to an end when centralised Christian monarchies were established in Scandinavia. The Vikings began to leave behind their traditions and customs in favour of a lifestyle much more similar to the rest of medieval Europe.

THE VIKINGS AS MERCHANTS

The life of a typical Viking followed the pattern of the seasons; agriculture in winter, travelling merchant in summer when the weather was more forgiving. For these Nordic populations, trade was essential to allow them to acquire goods which could not be found in Scandinavia such as silk, spices, wine or silver. In turn, the Vikings exported goods such as wood, wool, iron, honey, fish, tin and walrus ivory.

As such, the Vikings engaged in trade with Europeans, Arabs and the Slavic populations in Russia. However, in mainland Europe, some Christian merchants were reluctant to trade with them due to their Pagan beliefs. Nevertheless, the Vikings were not afraid to use force to obtain what they needed. Raids were an integral part of Norse customs; the Pagan pirates were happy to attack churches, convents, monasteries and other religious buildings which held great treasures and wealth. These raids also spread terror among the civilian populations who were not spared from this violence.

Viking trade was not always so bloody, with some Viking groups setting up more permanently in certain regions. Trading posts and farms were established in England, Scotland, Ireland and the Faroe Islands (a group of islands situated between Norway and the Northern Atlantic Ocean). This taste for travel and adventure became a Viking family tradition, with entire generations moving from country to country. Leif Eriksson's family was no different; in fact, they went further than most in this area.

THE VIKINGS AS EXPLORERS

While the rest of Europe's exploration ambitions lay in simply sailing away from the coastline to explore the oceans, the Vikings were travelling far and wide thanks to their excellent ships and unrivalled knowledge of the seas, built up throughout generations.

The Vikings are well-known for their *drakkars*, their legendary ships with dragon's heads carved into the wood at the bow and stern. Their technological prowess was largely due to a sound understanding of how their ships worked and an ability to maximise the potential of their equipment. They had two completely different types of boat which they employed at different times according to the goal at hand - either trade or war - and where the expedition was being led - either on rivers or the ocean:

- The Longboat: the warship, long and thin in its structure, was designed to sail on rivers. Its slim design made it more aerodynamic than most ships and helped it reach considerable speeds which aided the Vikings in their dawn raids and attacks.
- The Knarr: this seafaring vessel was completely different from the longboat. It was broader and heavier, more robust and capable of sailing the oceans. Its detachable sail helped it catch good winds and travel at a high speed for the era. This was the type of ship used by Eriksson and his crew to reach North America.

Other than their superior equipment, the Vikings were also masters of observation and orientation. They examined the heavens in minute detail, using the positions of the stars and the colour of the water and the sun to navigate the high seas. They were also known to release birds while at sea and follow them to the closest land. The Vikings were miles ahead of the rest of Europe; it was not until Henry the Navigator (Portuguese prince, 1394-1460) came along in the 15th century that Europeans would develop the technology and knowledge to allow them move away from the coasts and head for new lands.

THE EXPEDITION

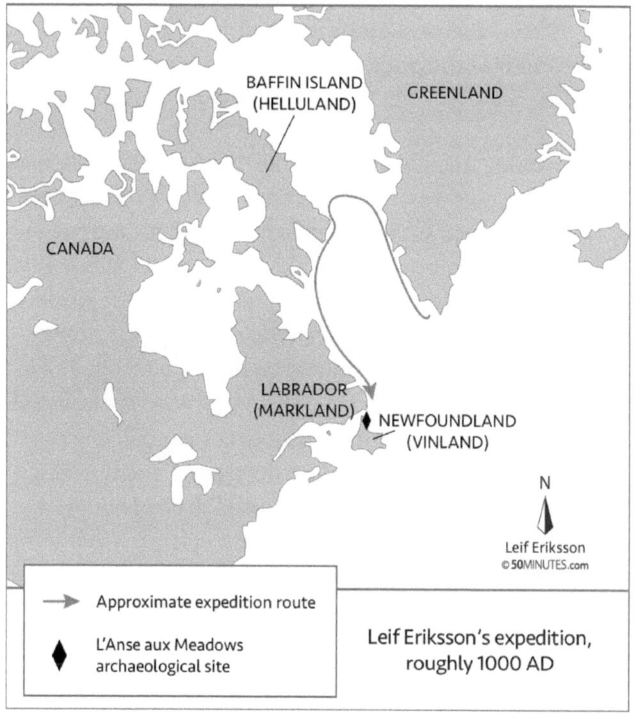

SEEKING A FORTUNE

Leif Eriksson's voyage of discovery, relayed in the Norse sagas, was the last step in a chain of westward colonisation led by the Eriksson family.

The idea of undertaking such a quest was planted in Eriksson's mind on his return from Norway when he heard talk of a new land, discovered by accident by a fisherman gone astray - Bjarni Herjolfsson. Leif Eriksson, son of Erik the red, viewed the potential rewards of this expedition as twofold:

- Discovering and colonising a new land would allow him to measure up to or even surpass his father and grand-father, who had set up colonies in Greenland and Iceland respectively. In echoing the achievements of those who went before him, Leif Eriksson would emerge glorious and ensure that his name went down in Viking history.
- Living conditions in Greenland were very difficult. The is-land is partially situated in the Arctic Circle; the hours of daylight are few in winter, it is extremely cold, and most importantly there are almost no trees. For the Vikings, wood was an essential resource, used to build houses and ships. Importing wood from Europe was very costly for the little Greenlandic colony. Discovering a new wooded territory which was closer to Greenland would be a major economic advantage.

Somewhere around the year 1000, Eriksson chose 35 men for his crew, including fisherman Bjarni Herjoltsson, to embark on a new voyage of discovery.

VIKING SUPERSTITION

The Vikings were extremely superstitious people, and Erik the Red was no exception to this rule. According to the Norse sagas, Leif Eriksson's father suddenly fell from his horse and injured his leg on his way to board the expedition ship. He read this as a bad omen and decided to stay in Greenland and give up his place among the crew.

THE VIKING SHIP EN ROUTE TO THE AMERICAS

The Norse sagas do not go into detail regarding Eriksson's actual voyage, only revealing that there were 35 crew-members and that the journey lasted for 6 days thanks to good winds. Despite it being fairly short, the voyage was not an easy one - they had to avoid icebergs and face high winds with only beer and cold food to eat throughout the journey.

Eriksson and his crew made several stops along the Canadian coastline before settling at a destination which took their liking. According to the sagas, the crew first came across a rocky and desolate land which they named Helluland (stone country) which could in fact have been modern day Baffin Island in Northern Canada. The crew did not settle here, likely due to the hostile environment on this freezing rocky region. Instead, they continued southward along the Labrador coastline. They landed there and named it Markland (forest country). Finally, the Vikings reached the land of their dreams after two more days of travelling and settled there for winter; this was Vinland.

Leif Erikson discovering America, painting by Christian Krohg, 1893.

The ocean-crossing was only possible due to the knarr ship itself, strong enough to sail far from the coastline and take on the ocean. In 1996, Danish captain Gunnar Marel Eggertsson sought to construct a replica model of a Viking ship using ancient techniques, aiming to study the ship's capacities and see if Eriksson's voyage would really have been possible. He used the remains and wreckage from old ships found by archaeologists as reference points for his construction. The boat was named *Islendingur*. At 22.5 m long and 5.3 m wide and weighing more than 18 tonnes, it was made using Scandinavian oak and more than 5000 nails.

The year 2000 marked 1000 years since Leif Eriksson discovered the Americas. To celebrate this, Eggerston decided to set sail on the *Islendingur* and replicate the journey made by Eriksson a whole millennium before. A crew of 9 men left Reykjavik, Iceland on 17 June 2000 and arrived in Newfoundland, Canada on 28 July. This was longer than Eriksson's original voyage because they made many stops along the way in Iceland, Greenland and Canada for commemoration ceremonies. The ship kept on sailing south and arrived in New York on 5 October 2000, though it is unlikely that any Viking ever set foot there.

VINLAND

After first landing in Helluland and Markland, Eriksson and his crew reached Vinland. It was here that they would spend the winter months to come, the land having multiple benefits and advantages. The days were longer in winter and its temperatures were higher than Greenland. Furthermore, the rivers were full of salmon and the forests were home to game for hunting. Above all, Vinland offered the Vikings the material they sought first and foremost: wood, used to build houses and ships. All these elements together proved very attractive to a group of men used to the freezing and unforgiving conditions of Greenland.

Where exactly did Eriksson and his crew explore? Through examining the descriptions given by the Vikings and the route they reportedly took, historians tend to agree that the crew first came across modern day Baffin Island, which they named Helluland, before sailing along the Labrador coasts - Markland - and settling in Vinland - modern Newfoundland. A Viking settlement was indeed discovered on the Anse aux

Meadows archaeological site in Newfoundland. The name Vinland is thought to mean "vine country", so-named by a crew-member who discovered grapevines there.

Despite this new land being rich in resources, Eriksson is said to have only spent a few months there before returning to Greenland - perhaps to take over his father Erik the Red's estate. Unfortunately, very little is known about the first European colony on American soil. The sagas do however report that two groups were formed among the Vikings, the first of which apparently stayed at the base to fish and hunt while the others set off to explore the surrounding area. Just how far the second group were able to venture is unknown, however certain historians have a theory that the Vikings went as far as the modern-day US border. This theory is supported by the discovery of butternuts - which come from a species of tree found only in Southern Canada and the North of the USA - in the L'Anse aux Meadows Viking settlement. However, no further evidence to prove that the Vikings went this far South has been discovered, meaning the theory remains unproven.

On Eriksson's return to Greenland, several groups of sett-lers composed of men, women and children reportedly set off for Vinland to reap the rewards of this fertile land. The sagas claim that the Viking settler populations came into contact with the indigenous Native American people of the territory. It is said that the two groups began trading until a dispute broke out and triggered a war between them. Terrified, the Vikings abandoned their new land and went back to Greenland. As such, after just a few years of occupation, the Vikings left the Americas and returned to the inhospitable territory of Greenland, giving up all hope of colonising the new land and establishing more permanent settlements there.

IMPACT

Few people knew about the Viking discovery of the Americas and it would probably have been totally forgotten if the Norse sagas were not there to record this achievement. How can it be that this major historical event went practically unnoticed, particularly compared to Columbus' "rediscovery" of America in 1492? Several factors help explain the mystery:

- A lack of financial resources to support the expedition. Leif Eriksson left his father's small colony in Greenland with a crew of just 35 men. His successor Columbus on the other hand, prepared his voyage with the financial support of the Spanish Crown. As such, the Vikings' material and financial resources were small in comparison.
- Their occupation of the territory was brief. Despite Vinland being rich in resources, the Vikings did not stay in North America for long. Only a few settlers came from Greenland to try their luck in this new land. Hostility quickly emerged between them and the Native American populations living there. The new arrivals quickly abandoned North America to return to Greenland, fearing for their lives. As such, the Viking colonisation was extremely brief in nature and bears no comparison to the monumental change engendered by Columbus' discovery a few centuries later. Armed with guns, the Spaniards took the continent by force and opened a pathway for intercontinental trade and the unrelenting European colonisation of the American continent.
- The Vikings were forgotten by the rest of the world. After

leaving for North America, the few Viking families who had been there returned to live in Greenland despite favourable conditions in Vinland. Erik the Red's colony in Greenland existed until the 13th century before it too was eventually abandoned. The existence of this remote region and its history was thus forgotten over the years by the rest of Europe. The same could have been said for the names Erik the Red and Leif Eriksson were it not for the Norse Sagas preserving their history. It was due to the rediscovery of these texts that the theory that the Vikings had discovered the Americas circulated once again among historians in the 19th century. It was not until 1960 that any evidence for this theory would be found. Ruins of a Viking settlement were found in L'Anse aux Meadows by Norwegian archaeologists Helge (1899-2001) and Anne Stine Ingstad (1918-1997). When analysis was conducted on the architectural remains and the archaeological material found on the site, it was confirmed that this was indeed a Viking and not a Native American settlement, as the local population had belie-ved. Furthermore, carbon-dating showed that it dated to around the year 1000, thus offering definitive proof of a Viking presence in North America.

Today, the USA and Scandinavia have both recognised Leif Eriksson's achievement and attribute to him not only the discovery of the Americas but also the place as the symbolic father of the large Scandinavian community in the USA. Congress decided to honour the great explorer and the entire Nordic-origin American population in an annual day of commemoration. Since 1964, Leif Eriksson day has been celebrated on 9 October. This date does not correspond to a specific event in Eriksson's life but was instead chosen to commemorate the day the ship Restauration, which transported many Norwegian immigrants, landed in New York on 9 October 1825.

SUMMARY

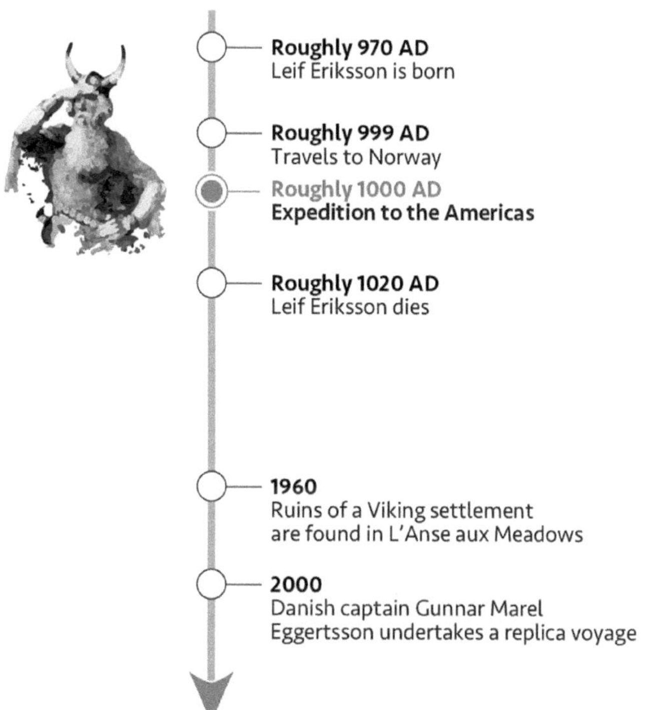

- Leif Eriksson was a Viking explorer who lived around the turn of the first millennium AD. He was the son of Erik the Red, who discovered and colonised Greenland.
- The lives and expeditions of these two men are outlined in the Norse Sagas, which recount the real or mythical stories of great Viking figures. These texts were written

several centuries after the events they detail actually took place, and occasionally present different accounts of the same story.

- Around 999, Eriksson embarks on his first voyage to Norway and converts to Christianity in King Olaf I's court. Under the king's influence, Eriksson accepts the challenge of taking Christian missionaries back to his homeland in the colony of Greenland.
- On hearing tales recounted by a fisherman who got lost at sea and caught sight of an unfamiliar land, Eriksson decides to set off in search of this new territory. He leaves Greenland in roughly 1000 AD and travels Westward in the hope of finding new resources such as wood, which could not be found in Greenland.
- The newly-found land is named Vinland due to the grapevines found there. This region of modern-day Newfoundland has bountiful natural resources. Eriksson spends just a few months there before returning to Greenland. Several families of settlers leave from Greenland for the new territory on his return.
- A small group reportedly continues to explore the region although no other Viking settlements have been found in the area.
- This little colony has a brief life-span and the Vikings returned home after just a few years, probably due to conflicts with the Native American populations.
- Leif Eriksson and the Vikings' presence in North America was forgotten for almost 1000 years until it was rediscovered by American historians and archaeologists thanks to the Nordic sagas.
- Today, the USA and Scandinavia have officially recognised

Eriksson's achievements. He is considered not only as the first European to set foot on American soil, but the founding father of the Scandinavian-origin community in the USA.

We want to hear from you!
Leave a comment on your online library
and share your favourite books on social media!

FIND OUT MORE

BIBLIOGRAPHY

* BBC. (2016) *History - Leif Ericson*. [Online]. [Accessed 17 May 2014.]. Available from: <http://www.bbc.co.uk/history/historic_figures/erikson_leif.shtml>
* BBC. (2016) *History – Vikings*. [Online]. [Accessed 17 May 2014.]. Available from: <http://www.bbc.co.uk/history/ancient/vikings>
* Boyer, R. (1978). *Les sagas islandaises*. Paris: Payot.
* Bozellec, A., Gravier, M. and Albertini, L. (1981) *La Saga d'Éric le Rouge. Contes Nordiques*. Paris: Gallimard.
* Morison, S. (1971) *The European Discovery of America. The Northern Voyages AD. 500-1600*. New York: Oxford University Press. Vol. 1.
* Unknown. (1978) Le Canada depuis 12 000 ans. Le Canada depuis l'origine : villages esquimaux, Indiens Iroquois, les Vikings et l'énigme du Vinland, les Français en Acadie, fouilles à Québec, les forteresses. *Les dossiers de l'archéologie*. Volume 27.
* Vinding, N. (1998) *The Viking Discovery of America (985 to 1008). The Greenland Norse and their Voyages to Newfoundland*. Madison: Edwin Mellen Press.

ICONOGRAPHIC SOURCES

* State of Leif Eriksson in Qassiarsuk, in the South of Greeland. Royalty-free reproduction picture.
* Painting showing Leif Eriksson just as he discovers Vinland. Royalty-free reproduction picture.

- *Leif Erikson discovering America*, painting by Christian Krohg, 1893. Royalty-free repdocution picture.

ADDITIONAL SOURCES

- Apps, R. and Marks, A. (1998) *The Sagas of Leif Erikson: Outlaw's Son.* Hove: Macdonald Young Books.
- Ingstad, H. (1969) *Westward to Vinland: The Discovery of Pre-Columbian Norse House-Sites in North America.* London: Jonathan Cape.
- Mackay Brown, G. (1992) *Vinland.* London: John Murray.
- Magnusson, V. (1965) *The Vinland Sagas: the Norse Discovery of America.* Baltimore: Penguin.

DOCUMENTARIES

- *The Vikings. Voyage to America.* (2006) [Documentary]. Brian Leckey. Dir. USA: The History Channel.

IMPROVE YOUR GENERAL KNOWLEDGE

IN A BLINK OF AN EYE !

www.50minutes.com

www.50minutes.com

ISBN ebook: 9782806279224

ISBN paper: 9782806282903

Legal Deposit: D/2016/12603/289

Cover: © Primento

Digital conception by Primento, the digital partner of publishers.